To the Teacher

The *Taking Off* Workbook provides supplementary practice for students who have basic reading and writing skills in their first language. Each *Taking Off* Workbook unit provides eight pages of supplementary exercises for its corresponding Student Book unit. The Workbook activities offer students further practice in developing the language, vocabulary, and life-skill competencies taught in the Student Book.

The Workbook also provides two pages of follow-up activities for each of the Grammar Spotlights presented throughout the Student Book.

Features

- **Wide range of exercises** can be used by students working independently or in groups, in the classroom, with a tutor, or at home.

- **New cast of characters** represents the same nationalities as the characters in the Student Book, but lends the Workbook a fresh set of faces.

- **Just for Fun** pages at the end of each unit feature word searches, crossword puzzles, and word scrambles.

- **Student Book page references** at the top of each Workbook page show how the two components support one another.

- **Correlation table at the back of the Workbook** helps teachers quickly cross-reference the Workbook and Student Book.

Cast of Characters

The *Taking Off* Student Book features an international cast of characters representing key countries from which many learners come. A second set of characters representing the same set of nationalities is introduced in the Workbook. Here is a profile of the characters in the *Taking Off* Workbook.

Character	Nationality
Jane Craft (teacher)	American
Marco Diaz	Colombian
Kim Dorel	Haitian
Luna Gilbert	Brazilian
Soo Jin Kim	Korean
Lin Kwok	Chinese
Thomas Jover	Haitian
Eva Martinez	Colombian
Alex Reyes	Mexican
Ivan Stoli	Russian
Erik Mendez	Brazilian
Ly Tran	Vietnamese
Mei Wu	Chinese

Taking Off Literacy Workbook

A special *Taking Off* Literacy Workbook has been designed for literacy students enrolled in low beginning classes. Most low beginning students are true beginners in English who are literate in their first language. Literacy students, on the other hand, usually do not have fundamental first-language literacy skills. Literacy students often need specific instruction in letter formation and other fundamental reading, listening, and writing skills.

As teachers who have worked with mixed groups of literacy and low beginning students know, dealing simultaneously with the needs of each of these groups of learners is a great challenge. The Literacy Workbook offers a unique resource for teachers in such multi-level classes. Each Literacy Workbook unit provides essential support for key elements of the *Taking Off* Student Book. Working with or without a teacher's aide, literacy students can tackle basic reading, listening, and writing activities in the Literacy Workbook while students with literacy skills in their first language can take on the tasks in the Workbook.

The *Taking Off* Literacy Workbook is divided into two sections. Section One contains 30 pages of basic literacy and numeracy exercises. These exercises focus on identifying and writing both uppercase and lowercase letters and the numbers 0–10. Section Two contains four pages of literacy support for each unit in Student Book. A special audiocassette/CD for the Literacy Workbook offers additional listening practice for literacy students.

Taking Off

Workbook

Susan Hancock Fesler
Christy M. Newman

Workbook Writer: Mari Vargo

McGraw-Hill
Contemporary

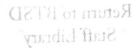
Taking Off Workbook: Beginning English, First Edition

 This book is printed on recycled, acid-free paper containing 10% postconsumer waste.

1 2 3 4 5 6 7 8 9 0 QPD 0 9 8 7 6 5 4 3 2 1

ISBN 0-07-282064-0
Editorial director: Tina B. Carver
Senior managing editor: Erik Gundersen
Developmental editor: Linda O'Roke
Director of North American marketing: Thomas P. Dare
Director of international sales and marketing: Kate Oakes
Production manager: Genevieve Kelley
Interior designer: Eileen Wagner
Art: Anna DiVito, Phil Scheuer, and Leap'n Lizards Design

**McGraw-Hill
Contemporary**

www.mhcontemporary.com

Table of Contents

Table of Contents

Table of Contents

Table of Contents

Table of Contents

Unit 1

Welcome to the Classroom

Welcome!

A **Complete.**

| ~~Jane~~ | meet | Nice | Soo Jin |

Jane: Hello, I'm _____Jane_____.

Soo Jin: Hi, Jane. I'm Soo Jin. Nice to _____ you.

Jane: _____ to meet you too, _____.

B **Complete.**

| Alex | China | from | ~~Hi~~ | I'm |

Alex: _____Hi_____. I'm _____. I'm _____ Mexico.

Mei: Hello. My name is Mei. _____ from _____.

C **Write your name.**

HELLO!
My name is

_____

The alphabet

A **Complete.**

A B C D __ F G __ __ J K L __

a __ c __ e f __ __ i j __ l m

B **Complete.**

N O __ Q __ S __ U V __ X __ Z

n __ p q __ __ t __ v w __ y __

C **Complete.**

first	How	last	spell	~~What's~~

Eva: Hello. I'm Eva Martinez. _____What's_____ your name?

Ivan: My name is Ivan Stoli.

Eva: _____ do you _____ that?

Ivan: My _____ name is I-V-A-N.

My _____ name is S-T-O-L-I.

D **Complete the sentences about you.**

My first name is _____.

My last name is _____.

What's in the classroom?

A **Complete.**

| backpack board book chair desk |
| door pen student teacher |

1. __backpack__   2. _____   3. _____

4. _____   5. _____   6. _____

7. _____   8. _____   9. _____

A   Circle.

a. book   **b.** backpack   **c.** pen   **d.** notebook

B   Check.

____ **a.** pen   ____ **b.** paper   ____ **c.** notebook   ____ **d.** board

C   Complete.

My name is _____.

D   Match.

1. __b__ desk

   a.

2. ____ computer

   b.

3. ____ paper

   c.

4. ____ door

   d.

Circle.

1. Open the book.

2. Close the book.

3. Point to the board.

4. Go to the board.

 **Check.**

1. __✔__ **a.** Close the door.

_____ **b.** Point to the door.

_____ **c.** Close the book.

2. _____ **a.** Put away the book.

_____ **b.** Point to the paper.

_____ **c.** Put away the paper.

3. _____ **a.** Take out the pen.

_____ **b.** Take out the book.

_____ **c.** Take out the paper.

A Write.

eight	five	four	nine	~~one~~	seven	six	ten	three	two

1	2	3	4	5
one	_____	_____	_____	_____

6	7	8	9	10
_____	_____	_____	_____	_____

B Write the numbers.

1. __1__ one

2. _____ nine

3. _____ seven

4. _____ four

5. _____ two

6. _____ five

C Complete.

address	e-mail address	~~phone number~~

1. My _____phone number_____ is 518-555-7036.

2. My _____ is 234 Elm Street.

3. My _____ is db107@freemail.com.

A Complete the form about you.

MCC **MARINA**
Community College

Your Name: _____
          First Name   Last Name

IN AN EMERGENCY:

Please Call: _____
          First Name   Last Name

_____
Phone Number

B Write the names of four students in your class.

Example: _Jose Cruz_____

1. _____

2. _____

3. _____

Just for fun

A **Unscramble the letters. Write the words.**

1. e m a n _____name_____

2. e l l h o _____

3. y m _____

4. i h _____

5. p e s l l _____

6. o a b d r _____

7. i c e n _____

8. a p p r e _____

B **Find the words.**

~~board~~ book chair computer desk
notebook paper pen student teacher

e	t	c	v	b	c	p	c	r	b	p	n	s
n	t	e	a	c	h	e	r	r	o	a	e	d
p	e	d	s	n	a	m	h	r	q	p	e	n
l	k	y	g	i	i	a	a	o	d	e	s	k
v	e	b	o	a	r	d	i	b	x	r	t	w
p	c	o	t	b	s	j	l	b	w	v	u	m
c	n	o	t	e	b	o	o	k	o	o	y	j
d	e	k	m	t	s	r	b	i	o	a	r	d
r	h	r	a	p	e	b	n	e	t	h	w	h
w	h	a	s	t	u	d	e	n	t	h	u	r
l	e	r	t	g	o	t	h	t	s	l	n	o
a	r	s	y	b	n	d	e	s	l	f	g	o
s	t	u	n	o	t	e	b	r	p	a	p	r

Workbook Lessons	Workbook Pages	Student Book Pages
Where are you from?	11	15
What language do you speak?	12	16
What language does he speak?	13	17
She is married.	14	18
I am average height.	15	19-21
What's your address?	16	22
Identification Form	17	23
Just for fun	18	

A Complete.

Alex: I'm from _____Mexico_____. Where are you from?

Mei: I'm from _____.

B Complete.

~~Alex~~ China Mei Mexico

A: Where is _____Alex_____ from?

B: He's from _____.

A: Where is _____ from?

B: She's from _____.

C Complete about you.

I'm from _____.

A Complete.

Ivan: I speak _____Russian_____. What language do you speak?

Soo Jin: I speak _____.

B Complete.

do	Spanish	~~speak~~	What

Mei: I _____speak_____ Chinese. _____ language

_____ you speak?

Marco: I speak _____.

C Complete about you.

My name is _____. I'm from _____.

I speak _____.

Read.

Name	Country	Language
Alex	Mexico	Spanish
Mei	China	Chinese
Marco	Colombia	Spanish
Luna	Brazil	Portuguese
Ly	Vietnam	Vietnamese

B **Complete.**

1. **A:** Marco is from _____Colombia_____. What language does he speak?

   B: He speaks _____.

2. **A:** _____ is from Vietnam. What language does she speak?

   B: She speaks _____.

3. **A:** Luna is _____ Brazil. What language does _____ speak?

   B: She _____ Portuguese.

4. **A:** _____ is from Mexico. What _____ does he speak?

   B: He speaks _____.

5. **A:** Mei is from _____. What language _____ she speak?

   B: She speaks _____.

She is married.

 Circle.

1. (**a.** married) **b.** single **c.** divorced **d.** widowed

2. **a.** married **b.** single **c.** divorced **d.** widowed

3. **a.** married **b.** single **c.** divorced **d.** widowed

 Complete.

divorced	married	single	~~widowed~~

1. Eva is ____widowed____.   2. Mary and Kim are _____.

3. Alex is _____.   4. Marco is _____.

I am average height.

A **Complete.**

Soo Jin   Alex   Lin   Mei

average height	short	~~tall~~	tall

1. Lin is _____ tall _____.

2. Soo Jin is _____.

3. Alex is _____.

4. Mei is _____.

B **Write about the people.**

Soo Jin   Alex   Mei

don't wear	wears

1. Soo Jin _____ glasses.

2. Alex and Mei _____ glasses.

A Complete.

eighteen	~~eleven~~	fifteen	fourteen
nineteen	seventeen	sixteen	thirteen	twelve

11	12	13	14	15
eleven	_____	_____	_____	_____

16	17	18	19
_____	_____	_____	_____

B Write the numbers.

1. _____ eleven   3. _____ fourteen   5. _____ fifteen

2. _____ nineteen   4. _____ sixteen   6. _____ twelve

C Complete.

address	My	~~What's~~	your	zip code

A: _____What's_____ your _____?

B: _____ address is 324 Short Street.

A: What's _____ zip code?

B: My _____ is 92924.

D Complete about you.

My address is _____.

My zip code is _____.

A Complete the form for Luna.

Hi. My name is Luna J. Gilbert. I'm widowed. I have brown eyes. I have black hair. My address is 324 Lake Street. My zip code is 12183. I live in Troy, NY.

IDENTIFICATION FORM

TYPE OR PRINT

Gilbert

| LAST NAME | FIRST NAME | MI |

| ADDRESS | CITY | STATE | ZIP |

CIRCLE ONE:

| MARITAL STATUS: | SINGLE | MARRIED | DIVORCED | WIDOWED |

| EYE COLOR: | BLUE | BROWN | GREEN | BLACK |

| HAIR COLOR: | BROWN | BLACK | WHITE | RED | BLOND |

A Complete.

Chinese	~~English~~	Korean	Portuguese
Russian	Spanish	Vietnamese	

1. I'm from the USA. I speak _____ English _____.

2. I'm from Mexico. I speak _____.

3. I'm from Brazil. I speak _____.

4. I'm from Vietnam. I speak _____.

5. I'm from Korea. I speak _____.

6. I'm from Russia. I speak _____.

7. I'm from China. I speak _____.

B What are the words?

Across

3. My _____

is 23 Paper Street.

6. _____. I'm Mei.

Down

1. My _____ is Alex.

2. Nice to _____ you, too.

4. How do you _____ that?

5. What's _____ name?

Complete.

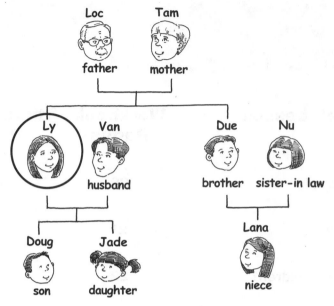

Loc — father
Tam — mother
Ly
Van — husband
Due — brother
Nu — sister-in law
Doug — son
Jade — daughter
Lana — niece

1. Kim: What's your husband's name?

   Ly: His name is _____ *Van* _____.

2. Kim: What's your mother's name?

   Ly: Her name is _____.

3. Kim: What's your father's name?

   Ly: His name is _____.

 Complete. Look at the pictures in Activity A.

| ~~brother~~ daughter niece sister-in-law |

1. Due is Ly's _____ brother _____.

2. Lana is Ly's _____.

3. Jade is Ly's _____.

4. Nu is Ly's _____.

Look at the pictures on page 20. Complete.

1.

   Loc

   A: Who is Loc?

   B: _____ Loc _____ is Ly's _____.

2.

   Tam

   A: Who is _____?

   B: _____ is Ly's mother.

3. Doug

   A: _____ is Doug?

   B: Doug is Ly's _____.

Read and check. Look at the pictures on page 20.

1. Who is Loc?

✔ Ly's father.

____ Ly's brother.

2. Who is Lana?

____ Ly's mother.

____ Ly's niece.

3. Who is Tam?

____ Ly's father.

____ Ly's mother.

4. Who is Doug?

____ Ly's husband.

____ Ly's son.

5. Who is Nu?

____ Ly's niece.

____ Ly's sister-in-law.

6. Who is Van?

____ Ly's husband.

____ Ly's brother.

A Complete.

| a | ~~children~~ | daughter | Do | don't | I | No |

Soo Jin: Do you have ___children___?

Ly: Yes, I have a son and a _____.

Kim: No, I _____.

Alex: _____ you have children?

Jane: _____, I don't.

Luna: Yes, _____ have _____ son.

B Write about you.

A: Do you have children?

You: _____.

Mr., Mrs., and Ms.

 Write *Mr.*, *Mrs.*, or *Ms.* Look at the picture on page 20.

Van

1. _____Mr._____ Van Tran

Loc   Tam

2. _____ and _____ Cao

Jade

3. _____ Jade Tran

Nu

4. _____ or _____ Nu Cao

Doug

5. _____ Doug Tran

Unit 3 **23**

A ## Complete Ivan's family tree.

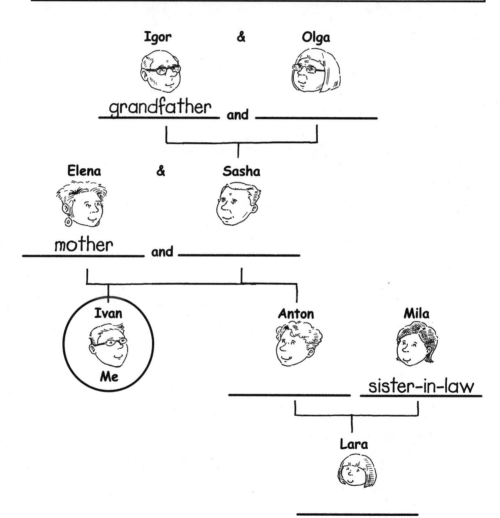

Igor   &   Olga

<u>grandfather</u> and _____

Elena   &   Sasha

<u>mother</u> and _____

Ivan
Me

Anton   Mila

_____ <u>sister-in-law</u>

Lara

_____

 B ## Write *middle-aged, old,* or *young*.

1. Ivan's niece is _____ *young* _____.

2. Ivan's grandfather is _____.

3. Ivan's father is _____.

A Write the numbers.

1. __90__ ninety

2. _____ fifty

3. _____ thirty

4. _____ one hundred

5. _____ sixty

6. _____ twenty-two

7. _____ seventy

8. _____ forty

9. _____ fifty

10. _____ eighty

B Write the numbers.

__20__ ____ ____ __50__ ____ ____ __80__ ____ __100__

C Complete.

| How | ~~old~~ | years | you | 68 |

Soo Jin: How _____old_____ are you, Luna?

Luna: I'm 52 _____ old.

Luna: _____ old are _____, Eva?

Eva: I'm _____ years old.

D Write about you.

A: How old are you?

You: I'm _____.

A Read about Alex's family.

Alex P. Reyes lives with his parents, Juan R. Reyes and Anita L. Reyes.
He also lives with his wife, Linda T. Reyes, and his daughter, Lola J. Reyes.
Alex lives with his son Ben S. Reyes, too.

Alex is 48. Juan and Anita are 70. Linda is 46. Lola is 17. Ben is 15.

The family's address is 178 Old Street in Albany, NY, 12203.

B Complete Alex's census form.

Census Form

Address: | 178 Old Street |

| | | |
| City | State | Zip Code |

List all the people at your address.

Mr./Mrs./Ms. First Name	MI	Last Name	Age
1. Mr. Alex	J.	Reyes	48
2.			
3.			
4.			
5.			
6.			

Complete.

brother	daughter	~~father~~	husband	mother	son

1. Your mother's husband is your f a t h e r .
                                      8   5

2. Your girl child is your ___ ___ ___ ___ ___ ___ ___ ___.
                                  3   10   4

3. Your daughter's brother is your ___ ___ ___.
                                        6

4. Your mother's son is your ___ ___ ___ ___ ___ ___ ___.
                                                          9

5. Your father's wife is your ___ ___ ___ ___ ___ ___.
                                   7   1

6. The man you are married to is your ___ ___ ___ ___ ___ ___ ___.
                                           2

B **Write the letters from Activity A.**

Y ___ ___ ___ ___ e ___ ___ a ___ ___!
   1   2   3   4   5   6   7   8 9 10

A Pronouns

Circle the pronouns.

(I) am Ly. I am from Hue, Vietnam. I speak Vietnamese and English. I am married. I have a brother and a sister-in-law. They speak Vietnamese and English, too. We live in the United States. I have a husband. He is from Vietnam, too. We have two children.

B Present tense of *BE*

Write *am*, *is*, or *are*.

1. Mei _____is_____ short.

2. Lin and Alex _____ tall.

3. I _____ average height.

4. They _____ young.

5. We _____ middle-aged.

6. Luna and I _____ old.

Write *'m*, *'s*, or *'re*.

1. He ___'s___ from China.

2. We _____ from Brazil.

3. They _____ from Colombia.

4. I _____ from Haiti.

5. She _____ from Vietnam.

6. I _____ from Russia.

7. You _____ from the USA.

8. She _____ from Mexico.

C *BE* with Negatives

Write negative sentences.

1. Juan is old. _____He's not_____ young.

2. Eva is middle-aged. _____ old.

3. Anton is young. _____ middle-aged.

4. Ivan and Mila are from Russia. _____ from the USA.

5. I'm from Colombia. _____ from Mexico.

6. Mei is from China. _____ from Vietnam.

7. Kim and Ivan are single. _____ married.

8. Alex and I are married. _____ single.

9. I'm divorced. _____ married.

D Present tense of *HAVE*

Write *have* or *has*.

1. Alex _____has_____ a brother.

2. Juan _____ two children.

3. Ly and Van _____ two children.

4. Luna _____ two brothers.

5. I _____ blue eyes.

6. Eva and Mei _____ black hair and brown eyes.

Unit 4 Welcome to our house

Workbook Lessons	Workbook Pages	Student Book Pages
He's in the kitchen.	31	43
Is there a lamp in the living room?	32	44
There's a shower in the bathroom.	33	45-46
I need a refrigerator.	34	47
Where do you study?	35	48-49
18 or 80?	36	50
A garage sale	37	51
Just for fun	38	

He's in the kitchen.

 A **Complete.**

| bathroom | bedroom | dining room |
| ~~kitchen~~ | living room | yard |

Lana and Ly

Doug

Jade

1. ____kitchen____ 2. _____ 3. _____

Loc

Van

Tam

4. _____ 5. _____ 6. _____

 B **Look at the pictures in Activity A. Complete.**

1. Lana and Ly are in the _____kitchen_____.

2. Loc is in the _____.

3. Jade is in the _____.

A Complete.

chair	in	No	~~there~~	Yes

Luna: Is _____there_____ a _____ in the living room?

Erik: _____, there is.

Luna: Is there a lamp _____ the kitchen?

Erik: _____, there isn't.

B Circle the answers.

1. A: Is there a fireplace in the living room?

   B: (Yes, there is.)   No, there isn't.

2. A: Is there a chair in the living room?

   B: Yes, there is.   No, there isn't.

3. A: Is there a bed in the bedroom?

   B: Yes, there is.   No, there isn't.

A   Circle.

1. There's a shower in the _____.   (bathroom)   kitchen

2. There's a closet in the _____.   hall   shower

3. There's a barbecue in the _____.   living room   yard

4. There's a refrigerator in the _____.   dining room   kitchen

5. There's a sink in the _____.   bathroom   bedroom

6. There's a window in the _____.   bedroom   yard

7. There's a tub in the _____.   kitchen   bathroom

B   Complete.

| ~~apartment~~   house   rented room |

Mei   Alex   Luna

1. __apartment__   2. _____   3. _____

C   Complete.

1. Luna lives in a _____rented room_____.

2. Mei lives in an _____.

3. Alex lives in a _____.

D   Write about you.

A: Where do you live?

You: I _____.

A Read.

Kim's new apartment

Eva's garage

Kim has a new apartment. She has some furniture. She needs more furniture. Eva has furniture for Kim. The furniture is in her garage.

B Complete.

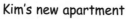

chair   desk   dresser   ~~lamp~~   sofa   table

Kim has a:	Kim needs a:
lamp	

C Complete.

lamp   need   Thanks   ~~What~~   you

Eva: _____ What _____ do _____ need?

Kim: I _____ a bed.

Eva: Do you need a _____ ?

Kim: No, I don't. _____ .

A Complete.

bathroom	bedroom	cook	kitchen
living room	~~shower~~	sleep	study

1. **A:** Where do you _____ shower _____?

   B: I shower in the _____.

2. **A:** Where do you _____?

   B: I cook in the _____.

3. **A:** Where do you study?

   B: I _____ in the _____.

4. **A:** Where do you _____?

   B: I sleep in the _____.

B Complete.

at the beach	in the city	in the country

1. _____   2. _____   3. _____

A **Write the numbers.**

1. ___30___ thirty   5. _____ twelve

2. _____ thirteen   6. _____ twenty

3. _____ eighteen   7. _____ ninety

4. _____ eighty   8. _____ nineteen

B **Write the words for the numbers.**

1. ___seventy___ 70   4. _____ 60

2. _____ 17   5. _____ 50

3. _____ 16   6. _____ 15

C **Write the numbers.**

1. There are _____20_____ apartments.
         twenty

2. The house is _____ years old.
         sixty

3. My address is _____ Pen Street.
         eighteen

4. There are _____ students in my class.
         fourteen

5. There are _____ chairs in my house.
         twelve

Match.

The students are at a garage sale. What do they need?

1. __e__ Soo Jin needs a bike.　　**a.**

2. _____ Ivan needs a lamp.　　**b.**

3. _____ Luna needs a fan.　　**c.**

4. _____ Thomas needs a backpack.　　**d.**

5. _____ Mei needs CDs.　　**e.**

Find the words.

| bed | chair | desk | dresser | fireplace | lamp | rug | sofa | table |

f	d	d	e	s	k	l	b	m	p
f	i	r	e	p	l	a	c	e	r
s	y	j	e	a	b	r	h	k	o
c	h	a	l	s	r	q	a	s	r
v	b	m	e	a	s	b	i	r	g
r	g	u	d	r	e	e	r	s	t
f	i	t	p	l	a	d	r	s	o
b	l	a	m	p	e	d	u	k	s
q	u	b	b	o	p	f	g	e	a
l	m	l	a	m	d	s	f	l	v
s	e	e	j	k	s	o	f	a	s
d	r	e	s	p	m	a	a	l	h

B **Write the words.**

1. **A:** Is there a ___shower___ ___ _____ bathroom?

                          h s o r e w   n i   h e t

   B: Yes.

2. **A:** Where _____ _____ parents?

                    r a e   o r y u

   B: They're in the kitchen.

Unit 5

I play soccer on Saturday.

Workbook Lessons	Workbook Pages	Student Book Pages
What do you do every day?	40	55
Days and months	41	56-57
What time is it?	42	58-59
Making an appointment	43	60
How often do you study?	44	61
Ordinal numbers	45	62
Completing a form	46	63
Just for fun	47	

What do you do every day?

A **Match.**

1. _c_ I play basketball.

2. ___ I watch TV.

3. ___ I read the newspaper.

4. ___ I work on my computer.

5. ___ I talk on the phone.

6. ___ I eat breakfast.

a.

b.

~~e.~~

d.

e.

f.

B **Complete.**

do	day	brush	~~What~~

Soo Jin: _____What_____ _____ you do every _____?

Eva: I _____ my teeth.

Days and months

A Complete the calendar.

Sunday	Monday	Tuesday
Wednesday	Thursday	Friday	Saturday

~~Sunday~~   Monday   Tuesday
Wednesday   Thursday   Friday   Saturday

Marco's Week

Sunday	_____	_____	_____	_____	_____	_____
12	**13**	**14**	**15**	**16**	**17**	**18**
garage sales study with Lin	English class	cook dinner study with Lin	English class	work	go to brother's house for dinner	play soccer with Alex

B Complete. Look at the calendar in Activity A.

1. Marco goes to garage sales on _____Sunday_____.

2. Marco goes to his brother's house on _____.

3. Marco and Lin study on _____ and _____.

4. Marco goes to English class on _____ and _____.

C Complete.

~~August~~ December February January March October

1. Aug. = _____August_____   4. Feb. = _____

2. Mar. = _____   5. Dec. = _____

3. Jan. = _____   6. Oct. = _____

A **Match.**

1. <u>b</u> 7:00   **a.** two fifteen

2. ___ 4:30   ~~**b.**~~ seven o'clock

3. ___ 2:15   **c.** four thirty

4. ___ 9:45   **d.** nine forty-five

B **Complete the sentences about Kim's day.**

1. Kim gets up at ____6:30____.

2. Kim showers at _____.

3. Kim eats breakfast at _____.

4. Kim goes to class at _____.

Making an appointment

A Complete.

appointment	at	Can	fine	~~like~~	make

Alex: I'd ___like___ to _____ an _____ for a tune-up.

Man: _____ you come on Monday at 7:00?

Alex: Monday at 7:00? That's _____ .

B Complete.

Eva: I'd like to make an appointment for a ___haircut___ .

Woman: Can you come on _____ at 3:45?

Eva: _____ at 3:45? That's fine.

Eva: I'd like to make an appointment for a cleaning.

Woman: Can you come on _____ at _____ ?

Eva: _____ at 10:30? That's fine.

A Complete.

How	month	often	Once

Luna: ___How___ _____ do you cook dinner?

Erik: _____ a week.

Eva: Every day.

Kim: Once a _____.

B Circle.

———— Thomas's month ————

Sunday	Monday	Tuesday	Wednesday	Thursday	Friday	Saturday
study English	study English	study English	study English	study English	study English	study English shop for food
study English	study English get a haircut	study English	study English	study English	study English	study English shop for food
study English	study English	study English	study English	study English	study English	study English shop for food
study English	study English	study English	study English	study English	study English	study English shop for food

1. Thomas shops for food _____. (once a week)   once a month

2. Thomas gets a haircut _____. once a week   once a month

3. Thomas studies English _____. every day   once a week

Ordinal numbers

STUDENT BOOK PAGE 62

 A **Match.**

1. _f_ 3rd   **a.** fifth

2. ___ 1st   **b.** second

3. ___ 5th   **c.** thirteenth

4. ___ 7th   **d.** eighth

5. ___ 2nd   **e.** fourteenth

6. ___ 8th   **f.** third

7. ___ 14th   **g.** first

8. ___ 13th   **h.** seventh

B **Write the numbers.**

1. ___9th___ ninth   7. _____ third

2. _____ eleventh   8. _____ seventh

3. _____ fourteenth   9. _____ eighth

4. _____ first   10. _____ sixth

5. _____ thirteenth   11. _____ ninth

6. _____ fifth   12. _____ twelfth

Completing a form

A Complete the chart for Eva.

> Hi. I'm Eva S. Martinez. I was born on September 6, 1959.

HILLTOP HEALTH CLINIC

Hilltop Health Clinic (518) 555-4567

Medical History

Martinez			
Last Name	First Name	MI	Date of Birth

B Complete Eva's calendar for this week.

> Sunday: garage sales
> Monday: cleaning
> Tuesday and Thursday: English class
> Wednesday: tune-up
> Saturday: basketball

Sunday	Monday	_____	_____	_____	Friday	_____
garage sales			tune-up			

Just for fun

 Complete.

1. March, _____April_____

A p r i l
13   4

2. _____, September

__ __ __ __ __ __
        5 11

3. December, _____

__ __ __ __ __ __ __
          6

4. _____, July

__ __ __
8 3

5. November, _____

__ __ __ __ __ __ __ __
12   2

6. September, _____

__ __ __ __ __ __ __
    7   9

7. January, _____

F e b r u a r y
    10

8. _____, April

__ __ __ __ __
   1

 Write the letters from Activity A. Answer the question.

W __ __ __   i __ __ __ __ __ __
   1 2 3   4 5   6 7 8 9

b __ __ __ __ __ a __ ?
10 4 9 11 1 12 13 6

It's in _____.

Unit 6

Let's go shopping.

I'm looking for a shirt.

A **Complete.**

| a coat | a dress | pants | a skirt |
| shoes | a suit | a sweater | a watch |

1. ___shoes___ 2. _____ 3. _____ 4. _____

5. _____ 6. _____ 7. _____ 8. _____

B **Complete.**

| ~~Excuse~~ | looking | me | Thank | watch |

Luna: _____Excuse_____ me. I'm _____ for a _____.

Clerk: Follow _____, please.

Luna: _____ you.

C **Complete.**

| help | I'm | jacket | ~~May~~ |

Clerk: _____May_____ I _____ you?

Alex: Yes, _____ looking for a _____.

Complete.

and	are	dress	I'm	~~What~~	wearing

Kim: _____What_____ are you _____ to the party?

Soo Jin: _____ wearing black pants _____ a

blue shirt. What _____ you wearing?

Kim: I'm wearing a purple _____.

Circle.

Clerk   Linda   Alex   Lola   Anita   Juan

1. Alex is wearing _____.   a suit   (pants and a shirt)

2. Linda is wearing _____.   pants   a skirt and a sweater

3. Lola is wearing _____.   pants   a skirt

4. Anita is wearing _____.   a blouse   a skirt

5. Juan is wearing _____.   a shirt   a sweater

6. The clerk is wearing _____.   a suit   a dress

A Complete the sentences.

blue	color	favorite	My	~~What~~

A: _____What_____ is your _____ color?

B: _____ favorite _____ is _____ .

B Complete the sentences.

Brown	color	dress	~~is~~	your

A: What color _____is_____ your _____?

B: Red.

A: What _____ are _____ shoes?

B: _____ .

C Write about your clothes.

A: What are you wearing?

You: I'm wearing _____ .

A: What color are your shoes?

You: _____ .

A: What color is your shirt?

You: _____ .

A **Match.**

1. _____ a small shirt

2. _____ a large skirt

3. _____ a medium jacket

a.

b.

c.

B **Write *small*, *medium*, or *large*.**

1. _____   2. _____   3. _____

C **Complete about you.**

A: What size are you?

You: I'm a _____.

A **Complete.**

Alex   Anita   Rita   Lola

too big	~~too long~~	too small	too small	too short

1. Alex's pants are _____ too long _____.

2. Alex's jacket is _____.

3. Rita's shoes are _____.

4. Lola's coat is _____.

5. Lola's pants are _____.

B **Write three sentences about Nick's clothes.**

1. Nick's pants are _____ too long _____.

2. Nick's shirt is _____.

3. Nick's jacket is _____.

Money

STUDENT
BOOK
PAGE 74

A Complete the chart.

25¢	~~1 cent~~	10 cents	a nickel	a quarter

1. a penny
__1 cent__
1¢

2. _____
5 cents
5¢

3. a dime
_____
10¢

4. _____
25 cents
_____

B Circle.

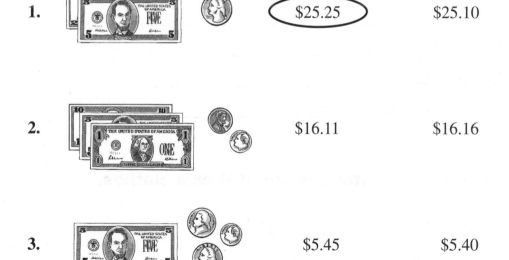

1. (\$25.25)   \$25.10

2. \$16.11   \$16.16

3. \$5.45   \$5.40

4. \$1.40   \$2.00

A Read.

It is February 14, 2005. Ivan is at Clark's Department Store. He is buying pants. The pants are $37.80. He is paying by check.

B Read.

It is December 20, 2005. You are at Sanford's Department Store. You are buying a sweater. The sweater is $26.05. Write a check.

C Complete.

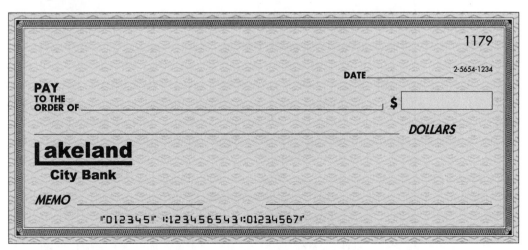

Just for fun

A **What are the words?**

Across

2. one cent = a _____

5. ten dimes = a _____

Down

1. two nickels = a _____

3. five cents = a _____

4. two dimes + one nickel = a _____

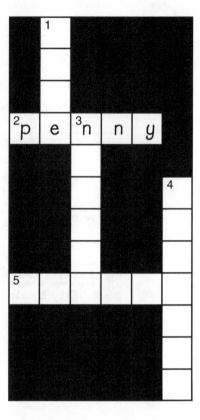

B **Find the words.**

coat	dress	pants	shirt	shoes	suit	sweater	watch

d	r	e	r	m	a	t	h	c
a	r	n	p	s	o	a	h	c
t	d	g	w	a	t	c	h	s
p	r	a	t	k	n	n	v	w
h	e	o	p	s	k	t	a	e
f	s	h	o	e	s	t	s	a
r	s	w	e	a	u	x	h	t
s	h	e	e	c	i	t	i	e
l	s	c	o	a	t	m	r	r
p	a	w	t	c	t	h	t	s

A Singular and Plural Nouns

Write the plural nouns.

1. I need a coat.

I need three _____coats_____.

2. I need a dress.

I need two _____.

3. I have a dollar.

I have four _____.

Circle the plural nouns.

Soo Jin, Eva, Kim, and Luna are at a garage sale. Soo Jin needs a bike. He also needs a desk. Eva needs (chairs) and a bed. Kim needs CDs. She needs two fans and a backpack, too. Luna needs a dresser, a coat, and tables.

Mei and Marco are at the garage sale. Mei needs a table and chairs. She needs a dress. Marco needs shirts and pants. He needs a sofa and two lamps.

B A/an

Write *a* or *an*.

I'm looking for __a__ house. I live in _____ apartment. My apartment building has _____ elevator. It has _____ bedroom, _____ kitchen, and _____ bathroom.

I'm looking for _____ apartment with two bedrooms, _____ kitchen, _____ yard, _____ bathroom, and _____ living room.

Simple Present Tense

Complete.

1. (eat) I _____ eat _____ breakfast every day.

2. (cook) Marco _____ on Mondays.

3. (play) Eva _____ soccer on Saturdays.

4. (work) Linda and Alex _____ every day.

5. (need) My brother _____ a bike.

6. (shop) Kim _____ for food once a week.

7. (get) Jane _____ a haircut once a month.

8. (study) My husband and I _____ English every day.

9. (sleep) I _____ in the bedroom.

10. (talk) Ly _____ on the phone every day.

A Complete.

| apples | ~~carrots~~ | eggs | ice cream | milk | potatoes |

1. __carrots__

2. _____

3. _____

4. _____

5. _____

6. _____

B Complete.

| milk | need | right |

A: We _____ apples.

B: That's _____. We need _____, too.

I'm looking for milk.

A Match.

1. _e_ beef

a.

2. ____ bread

b.

3. ____ butter

c.

4. ____ cake

d.

5. ____ cheese

e.

6. ____ chicken

f.

7. ____ oranges

g.

B Complete.

| Aisle | bread | in | looking | ~~me~~ |

A: Excuse _____ _me_ _____. I'm looking for milk.

B: It's _____ Aisle 3.

A: Excuse me. I'm _____ for _____.

B: It's in _____ 4.

A **Complete.**

~~breakfast~~	dinner	do	eggs	have	I	usually

Kim: What do you have for ___breakfast___?

Eva: I usually have _____. Sometimes I have cereal.

Kim: What _____ you have for lunch?

Eva: I _____ have a sandwich. Sometimes I have a hot dog.

Kim: What do you have for _____?

Eva: I usually _____ fish. Sometimes _____ have chicken.

B **Match.**

1. _b_ It's 12:00 p.m.   **a.** Let's have dinner.

2. ___ It's 5:00 p.m.   ~~b.~~ Let's have lunch.

3. ___ It's 8:00 a.m.   **c.** Let's have breakfast.

C **Write about you.**

I have breakfast at _____. I usually have _____ for breakfast. I have lunch at _____. I usually have _____ for lunch. Sometimes I have _____. I have dinner at _____. I usually have _____ for dinner.

I'll have a tuna sandwich, please.

A Complete.

cherry pie	coffee	hamburger
~~pizza~~	soda	sandwich

1. ___pizza___   2. _____   3. _____

4. _____   5. _____   6. _____

B Complete.

else	have	I'll	~~May~~	soda

Server: _____May_____ I help you?

Soo Jin: Yes. I'll _____ a hamburger, please.

Server: Anything _____?

Soo Jin: Yes. _____ have a _____, too.

Do you have hamburgers for dinner?

A Complete.

do	don't	for	have	~~you~~

Ivan: Do _____*you*_____ have hamburgers for dinner?

Thomas: No, I _____ .

Ivan: Do you _____ pizza _____ dinner?

Thomas: Yes, I _____ .

B Complete.

Thomas   Ivan

breakfast	chicken	~~eggs~~	lunch

Thomas: Do you have _____*eggs*_____ for _____?

Ivan: Yes, I do. Do you have _____ for _____?

Thomas: Yes, I do.

A potluck dinner

 Read.

Luna is having a potluck dinner.

It's a party!

Come to a potluck dinner at Luna's house!

Friday night at 6:00.

Bring your favorite food from your country. You can bring fruit, vegetables, meat, drinks, or cake.

Let's eat interesting food and have fun!

B ✔ **Check *True* or *False*.**

	True	False
1. The potluck is at Luna's house.	✔	
2. A potluck is a party.		
3. Luna makes all the food.		
4. Many people bring food.		
5. The party is in the morning.		

C **Complete about you.**

A: What is your favorite food?

You: My favorite food is _____.

A Match.

1. <u>b</u> a bag

2. ___ a bottle

3. ___ a box

4. ___ a bunch

5. ___ a can

6. ___ a package

a.

~~b.~~

c.

d.

e.

f.

B Look at the containers in Activity A. Complete.

| bag | ~~bottle~~ | box | bunch | can | package |

1. a ____bottle____ of oil

2. a _____ of grapes

3. a _____ of rice

4. a _____ of sugar

5. a _____ of tomato soup

6. a _____ of cereal

A **Find the words.**

| apples | beef | bread | butter | cake | carrots |
| chicken | eggs | fish | milk | onions | oranges |

o	n	i	o	n	s	i	o	m	m	c	c
a	p	b	e	e	h	s	w	o	i	t	o
c	r	b	r	e	a	d	n	g	l	l	r
h	d	u	j	m	o	g	r	d	k	c	a
i	h	t	c	h	i	c	f	i	s	h	n
c	s	t	g	j	e	x	y	d	h	e	g
k	t	e	c	o	l	f	b	s	r	v	e
e	x	r	a	p	p	l	e	s	r	g	s
n	c	a	k	y	k	r	e	g	g	s	l
i	v	s	e	d	i	r	f	k	b	i	e
h	r	l	n	o	h	v	a	r	d	f	t
c	a	r	r	o	t	s	i	r	v	a	m

B **Write the words.**

1. a _____ of oil
   o t l t b e

2. a _____ of bananas
   u n b h c

3. a _____ of cereal
   x o b

4. a _____ of soda
   n c a

A Complete.

cold	hot	rainy	snowy	~~sunny~~	windy

1. It's ___sunny___. **2.** It's _____. **3.** It's _____.

4. It's _____. **5.** It's _____. **6.** It's _____.

B Complete.

cold	It's	Los Angeles	~~weather~~

Lola: How's the ___weather___ in New York?

Alex: It's _____. How's the weather in _____?

Lola: _____ hot.

A **Write the seasons.**

| winter | spring | ~~summer~~ | fall |

1. It's _____ summer _____.

2. It's _____.

3. It's _____.

4. It's _____.

B **Complete.**

| favorite | season | Spring | What's | ~~your~~ |

Eva: What's _____ your _____ favorite _____?

Ly: Summer. _____ your _____ season?

Eva: _____.

C **Write about you.**

A: What's your favorite season?

You: _____.

I'm playing soccer.

 Match.

1. _d_ playing soccer   **a.**

2. ___ watching TV   **b.**

3. ___ dancing   **c.**

4. ___ cooking   ~~**d.**~~

5. ___ reading   **e.**

6. ___ walking   **f.**

 Write.

Linda and Alex   Ly   Erik   Soo Jin

1. What are Linda and Alex doing? They're _____ dancing _____.

2. What's Ly doing? She's _____.

3. What is Erik doing? He's _____.

4. What's Soo Jin doing? He's _____.

A Complete.

~~do~~	doing	like	summer

Mei: What ____do____ you like _____ in the _____?

Ivan: I _____ swimming.

B Look at the pictures. Complete.

Kim   Thomas   Eva   Erik

1. Ly: What do you like doing in the _____spring_____?

    Kim: I like _____walking_____.

2. Ly: What do you like doing in the _____?

    Thomas: I like _____.

3. Ly: What do you like doing in the _____?

    Eva: I like _____.

4. Ly: What do you like doing in the fall?

    Erik: I like _____.

A **Write about the weather.**

| cloudy | ~~cold~~ | cold | hot | rainy | ~~snowy~~ | sunny | windy |

1. It's _____ cold _____

and _____ snowy _____ .

2. It's _____

and _____ .

3. It's _____ and

_____ .

4. It's _____ and

_____ .

What's the temperature?

A **Complete.**

| ~~30°~~ | 50° | 85° | 103° |

1. It's snowy and cold. It's _____30°_____ F.

2. It's very hot! Let's go to the beach. It's _____ F.

3. It's sunny and cloudy today. It's hot.
It's _____ F.

4. It's cold and windy today. It's _____ F.

Complete the chart.

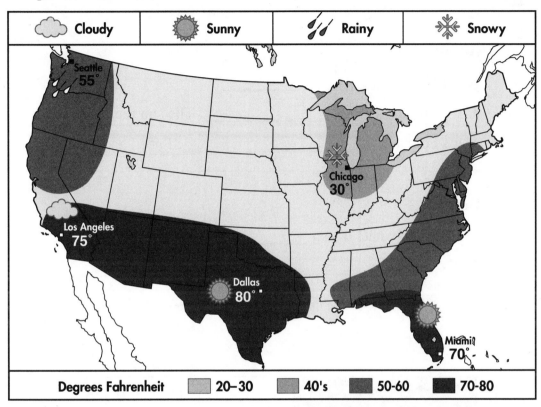

	Cloudy		Sunny		Rainy		Snowy

Seattle 55°

Chicago 30°

Los Angeles 75°

Dallas 80°

Miami 70°

Degrees Fahrenheit ☐ 20–30 ☐ 40's ☐ 50-60 ☐ 70-80

City	Temperature	Sunny	Rainy	Snowy	Cloudy
Seattle	55°F		✔		
Los Angeles					
Dallas					
Chicago					
Miami					

 Write a weather report for Dallas.

This is a weather report for Dallas.

A What are the words?

Across

1. How's the _____?

3. It's 70°F. It's _____. The sun feels good.

4. It's cold and it's _____. I need an umbrella.

Down

1. Oh no! My hat! It's so _____!

2. It's 101°F. It's _____.

3. It's cold and white outside. It's _____!

A Write the places.

| bank | fire station | gas station |
| hospital | ~~library~~ | police station |

1. __library__   2. _____   3. _____

4. _____   5. _____   6. _____

B Complete.

| bank | going | I'm | ~~Where~~ |

Thomas: ____Where____ are you _____?

Erik: _____ going to the _____.

Neighborhood map

 Write.

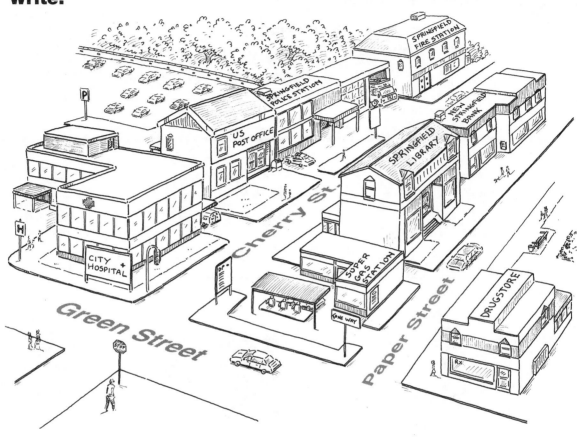

1. Man: Excuse me. Where's the post office?

Thomas: It's on ___Cherry Street___.

Man: Thanks.

2. Man: Excuse me. Where's the library?

Mei: It's on _____.

Man: Thanks.

3. Man: Excuse me. Where's the police station?

Marco: It's on _____.

Man: Thanks.

A Write the places.

bus stop	laundromat	movie theater
park	~~restaurant~~	supermarket

1. restaurant

2. _____

3. _____

4. _____

5. _____

6. _____

B Complete.

isn't	library	neighborhood	~~there~~

Ly: Is _____there_____ a restaurant in your neighborhood?

Nick: Yes, there is.

Ly: Is there a _____ in your _____?

Nick: No, there _____.

A Complete.

between	next to	~~drugstore~~	restaurant

Pedro: Where's the ____drugstore____?

Ly: It's _____ the post office and the _____.

Pedro: Where's the laundromat?

Ly: It's _____ the bank.

B Look at the picture in Activity A. Complete.

~~between~~	next to	on

1. The bank is ____between____ the laundromat and the movie theater.

2. The movie theater is _____ the restaurant.

3. The laundromat is _____ 1st Street.

A Complete.

do	don't	~~live~~	far from	you

Eva: Do you _____live_____ near a post office?

Kim: Yes, I _____.

Eva: Do _____ live _____ a bank?

Kim: No, I _____.

B Match.

Where do you...

1. _b_ buy stamps?

2. ___ watch a movie?

3. ___ wash clothes

4. ___ make a deposit?

a. At a laundromat.

b. At a post office.

c. At a bank.

d. At a movie theater.

C Write about you.

1. A: Do you live near a market?

You: _____.

2. A: Do you live far from a restaurant?

You: _____.

3. A: Where do you buy stamps?

You: _____.

Banking

 A **Read.**

Eva is putting money in the bank. She is depositing three checks into her savings account. This is her deposit slip.

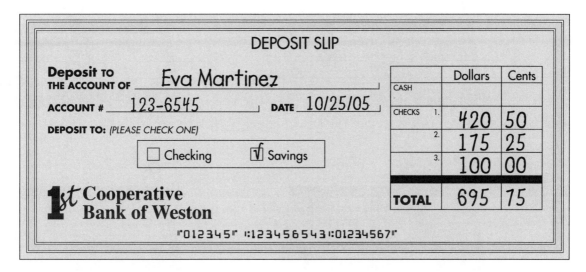

DEPOSIT SLIP

Deposit TO
THE ACCOUNT OF Eva Martinez

ACCOUNT # 123-6545   DATE 10/25/05

DEPOSIT TO: (PLEASE CHECK ONE)

☐ Checking   ☑ Savings

1st Cooperative
Bank of Weston

⑈012345⑈ ⑆123456543⑆01234567⑈

	Dollars	Cents
CASH		
CHECKS 1.	420	50
2.	175	25
3.	100	00
TOTAL	695	75

 B **Complete.**

1. The date is   October 25, 2005   .

2. Eva's account number is _____.

3. She is depositing $_____.

4. She is depositing money into her _____ account.

5. She is depositing _____ checks.

Using an ATM

A **Read.**

Soo Jin is using an ATM. He is taking money from his checking account. He's making a withdrawal.

1

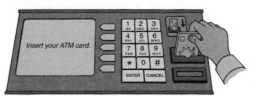

4

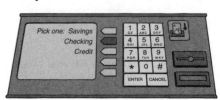

2

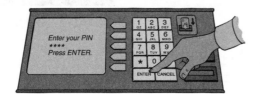

5

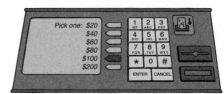

3

6

B **Circle.**

1. Soo Jin's PIN is 1256. He presses _____.   1278   (1256)

2. He is making a _____.   deposit   withdrawal

3. He is taking money from _____.   savings   checking

4. He is taking _____. $100.00 $40.00

A **Where do you...?**

1. Where do you watch a movie?

   At a <u>m</u> <u>o</u> <u>v</u> <u>i</u> <u>e</u>   <u>t</u> <u>h</u> <u>e</u> <u>a</u> <u>t</u> <u>e</u> <u>r</u>.
           8 9   1

2. Where do you wash your clothes?

   At a __ __ __ __ __ __ __ __ __.
               5

3. Where do you make a deposit?

   At a __ __ __ __.
        2

4. Where do you play soccer?

   At a __ __ __ __.
         7

5. Where do you buy aspirin?

   At a __ __ __ __ __ __ __ __.
        6   4

6. Where do you buy food?

   At a __ __ __ __ __ __ __ __ __ __.
            11   3

7. Where do you eat lunch?

   At a __ __ __ __ __ __ __ __ __.
       10

B **Write the letters from Activity A. Answer the question.**

W <u>h</u> __ __ ' __   y __ __ __   f __ <u>v</u> __ __ <u>i</u> __ __
   1 2 3 4   5 6 7   2 8 5 7 9 3 10

__ __ <u>v</u> <u>i</u> __ ?
11 5 8 9 10

It's _____.

Grammar Spotlight for Units 7-9

A Present Continuous

Write the present continuous.

1. Kim is in the library. _____She's studying_____.
   She/study

2. Soo Jin and Thomas are in the park. _____ soccer.
   They/play

3. Eva is in the supermarket. _____ milk and bread.
   She/buy

4. Alex is in the kitchen. _____ dinner.
   He/cook

5. Kim is in the bedroom. _____ on the phone.
   She/talk

6. The dog is in the yard. _____.
   It/play

7. Tam and Loc are in the restaurant. _____ dinner.
   They/eat

8. You and Lola are in the living room. _____ TV.
   You/watch

9. Marco and I are in the supermarket. _____ food.
   We/buy

10. Ivan is in the park. _____ the newspaper.
    He/read

B Question Words

Match.

1. __b__ What time is it?

2. ___ Where are Alex and Soo Jin?

3. ___ How are your children?

4. ___ Where's the gas station?

5. ___ What is your favorite color?

6. ___ How's the weather?

7. ___ What's your favorite movie?

8. ___ What's your name?

a. It's next to the bank.

b. 8:00.

c. Eva.

d. *Lord of the Rings.*

e. They're fine.

f. Yellow.

g. It's sunny.

h. They're in the park.

Write *How*, *Where*, or *What*.

<u>Questions</u>

1. ____Where____'s the bank? ⟶ Next to the post office.

2. _____ are your parents? ⟶ They're fine.

3. _____ are your parents? ⟶ In the yard.

4. _____'s your favorite food? ⟶ Pizza.

5. _____'s your class? ⟶ It's fine.

6. _____'s the beef? ⟶ Aisle 5.

7. _____'s your favorite color? ⟶ Blue.

8. _____ are Ly and Kim? ⟶ In the supermarket.

9. _____'s the weather? ⟶ It's raining.

10. _____ time is it? ⟶ 7:30.

<u>Answers</u>

Unit 10 You need to see a doctor.

Workbook Lessons	Workbook Pages	Student Book Pages
What's the matter?	89	123-124
My son is sick.	90	125
Health problems	91	126-127
I exercise.	92	128
They are healthy.	93	129
Taking medicine	94	130
Health insurance	95	131
Just for fun	96	

A Write.

| a cold | ~~a sore throat~~ | a stomachache |

1. a sore throat   2. _____   3. _____

B Write.

| finger   foot   ~~hand~~   leg |

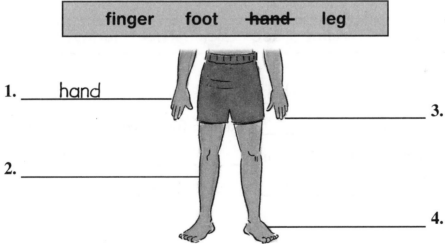

1. ___hand_____

2. _____

3. _____

4. _____

C Complete.

| arm   headache   ~~matter~~   with |

Mei: What's the ____matter_____?

Eva: I have a _____.

Mei: What's the matter _____ Marco?

Eva: His _____ hurts.

A Complete.

| bad | doctor | need | stomach |

Ben: I feel _____bad_____.

My _____ hurts.

Alex: You _____

to see a _____.

B Complete.

| fine | see | sick | This | Today |

Alex: Hello. _____This_____ is Alex Reyes. My son is

_____. Can Dr. Black see him today?

Woman: Yes. Dr. Black can _____ him at 8:30.

Alex: _____ at 8:30? That's _____. Thank you.

C Write.

Ben's _____stomach_____ hurts. He has an appointment to see Doctor Black

_____ at _____.

A Write.

a cut   a cough   ~~a fever~~   an infection

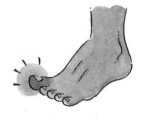

1. __a fever__   2. _____   3. _____   4. _____

B Complete.

an antibiotic   ~~aspirin~~   a bandage   cough syrup

1. Ivan has a fever. He needs _____ aspirin _____.

2. Ly has an infection. She needs _____.

3. Mei has a cough. She needs _____.

4. Thomas has a cut. He needs _____.

C Complete.

bad   bandage   ~~has~~   needs

Soo Jin: Luna _____ has _____ a cut on her leg.

Eva: That's too _____. She _____ a

_____.

A **Match.**

1. _C_ I exercise.

a.

2. ___ I drink a lot of water.

b.

3. ___ I eat healthy food.

~~c.~~

4. ___ I get enough sleep.

d.

B **Complete.**

| Jump. | Raise your arms. | ~~Stretch.~~ | Touch your toes. |

1. _____Stretch._____

2. _____

3. _____

4. _____

They are healthy.

 A **Read.**

Lin is 44 years old. Her mother May is 74 years old. Lin and May are healthy. They exercise every day. They like to walk in the park every day at 9:00 a.m. Once a week, Lin plays soccer. May dances once a week.

Lin and May eat healthy food. Lin likes carrots. May likes apples.

B **Complete the diagram.**

dances   eats healthy food   exercises every day
~~healthy~~   44   likes apples   likes carrots
74   plays soccer   walks in the park

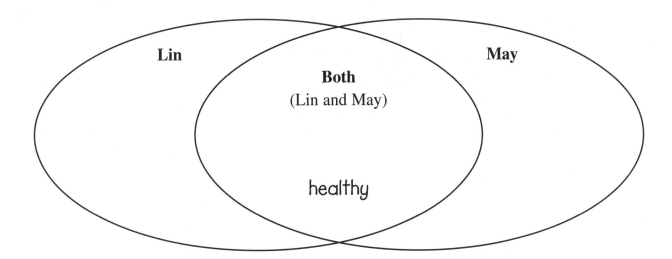

C **Write about you.**

1. I _____ every day.

2. I _____ once a week.

Taking medicine

A **Read.**

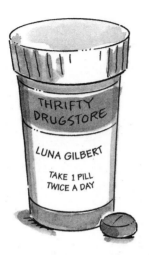

B **Circle.**

Medicine for:	It's a _____ .	Take ____ a day.
Luna	(pill) capsule teaspoon of medicine	1x 2x 3x
Lola	pill capsule teaspoon of medicine	1x 2x 3x

Read.

    Lin has a health insurance card. She needs the card to see a doctor. Her health insurance is from her husband's work. Her husband's name is Hong.

B **Fill in the form for Lin.**

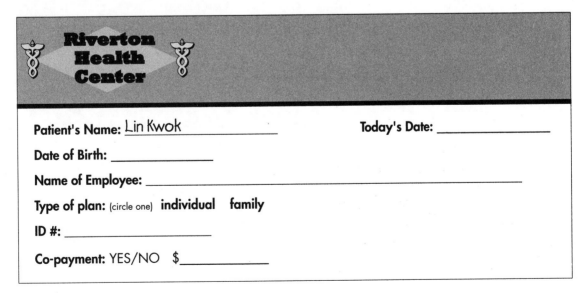

Just for fun

A Find the words.

~~ankle~~	arm	eye	finger	foot
hand	head	leg	nose	stomach

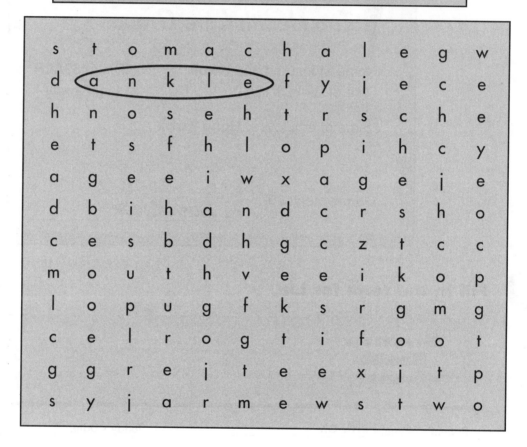

```
s   t   o   m   a   c   h   a   l   e   g   w
d   a   n   k   l   e   f   y   j   e   c   e
h   n   o   s   e   h   t   r   s   c   h   e
e   t   s   f   h   l   o   p   i   h   c   y
a   g   e   e   i   w   x   a   g   e   j   e
d   b   i   h   a   n   d   c   r   s   h   o
c   e   s   b   d   h   g   c   z   t   c   c
m   o   u   t   h   v   e   e   i   k   o   p
l   o   p   u   g   f   k   s   r   g   m   g
c   e   l   r   o   g   t   i   f   o   o   t
g   g   r   e   j   t   e   e   x   j   t   p
s   y   j   a   r   m   e   w   s   t   w   o
```

B Write the words.

1. e r S t t h c

Stretch

2. p m J u

3. a s i R e

4. o u c h T

A Write the jobs.

cashier custodian delivery person
gardener waiter

1. ____cashier____   2. _____   3. _____

4. _____   5. _____

B Complete.

cook ~~do~~ I'm person

Erik: What _____do_____ you do?

Mei: _____ a delivery _____. And you?

Erik: I'm a _____.

A ✔ **Check who uses it.**

Jobs	A telephone	A cash register	Pots and pans	A broom
receptionist	✔			
cook				
cashier				
custodian				

B **Complete.**

1. A _____receptionist_____ uses a telephone.

2. A _____ uses pots and pans.

3. A _____ uses a broom.

C **Complete the chart.**

Jobs	Indoors	Outdoors	With People	With Machines
waiter	✔		✔	
gardener				
receptionist				
delivery person				
taxi driver				

A Write.

drive	fix	~~sell~~	use

1. ___sell___   2. _____   3. _____   4. _____

B Complete.

And	computer	fix	~~What~~	you

Luna: _____What_____ can _____ do?

Ly: I can _____ things. _____ you?

Luna: I can use a _____.

C Complete.

can't	car	use	Yes	~~you~~

Marco: Can _____you_____ drive a _____?

Alex: _____, I can. Can you _____ a computer?

Marco: No, I _____.

Reading want ads

 A **Read and circle the jobs.**

1.
Can you drive?

 taxi driver

Call 555-0044
Star Taxi Company

2.
Green Trees, Inc.

needs a gardener.
Part time.

**Call the manager,
Ms. Flower 555-1245**

3.
WANTED:
**Experienced
Custodian**

**White Industries
1717 4th Street**

Call Bob Sacks,
the manager,
at 555-9023

4.
**KING
COMPUTERS**

727 State Street
555-9929

**full time receptionist
wanted**
$18/hour

B **Match.**

1. _b_ Who do you call at Green Trees, Inc.?   **a.** 1717 4th Street

2. ___ What is the phone number at Green Trees, Inc.?   ~~**b.**~~ Ms. Flower

3. ___ What is the address of King Computers?   **c.** 555-0044

4. ___ What is the phone number at Star Taxi Company?   **d.** 727 State Street

5. ___ What is the address of White Industries?   **e.** 555-1245

C **Read. Write the ad number from Activity A.**

Lin: I was at Banana House for five years. I was a custodian.

Soo Jin: I like plants and flowers. I want to be a gardener.

Eva: I can type. I am a receptionist.

Thomas: I want the taxi driver job.

1. Lin: _____3_____   **3.** Eva: _____

2. Soo Jin: _____   **4.** Thomas: _____

A **Write.**

before	I	job	taxi driver	~~was~~

Lin: I _____was_____ a salesclerk in Hong Kong.

What was your _____ before?

Marco: I was a waiter in Colombia.

Luna: _____ was a receptionist in Brazil.

What was your job _____, Thomas?

Thomas: I was a _____ in Haiti.

B **Read.**

Lin Kwok's address is 474 Jones Street, Troy, NY 12183. Her telephone number is 518-555-6263. She was a salesclerk at Kane's Department Store from 1990-1997.

C **Complete the form for Lin Kwok.**

Personal Data Sheet ▬▬▬

Name: Lin Kwok _____

Address: _____

Telephone: _ _ _ - _ _ _ - _ _ _ _

Work Experience:

Job	Employer	Dates

A Read.

Jake's Restaurant		1379
	Date 2/22/05	

Amount ONE HUNDRED EIGHTY-SEVEN DOLLARS AND FORTY-EIGHT CENTS $187.48

PAY TO THE ORDER OF Ivan Stoli

Cara Colla

Ivan Stoli	1379
Pay Rate:	$10/hour
Hours:	25
Gross Pay:	$250

Deductions	
Federal Tax:	$44.48
State Tax:	$10.95
FICA:	$2.97
Medicare:	$3.62
Total Deductions	$62.52

B Circle.

1. The paycheck is for _____.   (Ivan Stoli)   Cara Colla

2. Ivan works at _____.   Jake's restaurant   Cara Colla

3. Ivan works for _____.   20 hours   25 hours

4. Ivan's paycheck is for _____. $250.00 $187.48

5. Ivan's federal taxes are _____. $62.52 $44.48

6. Ivan's state taxes are _____. $10.95 $44.98

C Write.

Ivan takes the check to the bank. He makes a deposit of $_____.

A Read.

Luna J. Gilbert's address is 324 Lake Street, Troy, NY, 12183. Her telephone number is 518-555-1572. She was a cook at Lucky Restaurant from 1987–2001.

B Complete the form for Luna.

JOHNSON'S DEPARTMENT STORE Employment application

Gilbert
LAST NAME   FIRST NAME   MI

ADDRESS   CITY   STATE   ZIP

Telephone Number: (_ _ _) _ _ _ - _ _ _ _

Work Experience: _____

Employer: _____

Years of Experience: _____

What are the words?

Across

1. I work in a restaurant. I make food. I'm a _____.

5. I work in an office. I answer the telephone. I'm a _____.

6. I work with trees and flowers. I'm a _____.

Down

1. I work in a store. I take money from people. I'm a _____.

2. I work in a car. I drive every day. I'm a _____.

3. I clean offices and I fix things. I'm a _____.

4. I work in a restaurant. I give people food. I'm a _____.

I take a bus.

 Write.

| ~~drive a car~~   ride a bike   take a bus   take a subway |

1. _____drive a car_____

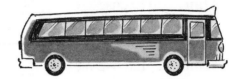

2. _____

3. _____

4. _____

B **Complete.**

| drive   ~~ride~~   take   walk |

Marco: How do you get to school?

Ivan: I _____ride_____ a bike.

Thomas: I _____ a car.

Lin: I don't have a car. I _____.

Alex: I _____ a bus.

A Complete.

ahead between ~~me~~ post office Where

Man: Excuse _____me_____ . Where is the _____?

Eva: It's straight _____.

Woman: Excuse me. _____ is the restaurant?

Eva: It's _____ the drugstore and the library.

B Circle the answers.

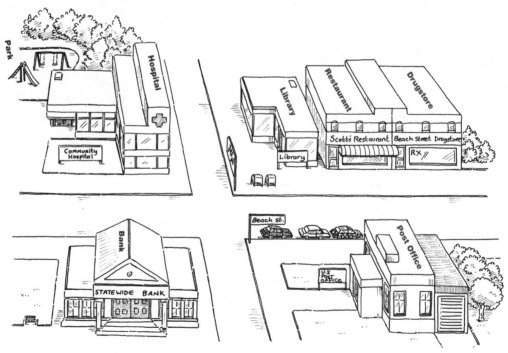

1. Where is the hospital?

It's between the bank.   (It's across from the bank.)

2. Where is the post office?

It's across from the park.   It's across from the restaurant.

3. Where is the park?

It's next to the hospital.   It's between the library and the drugstore.

How do I get to the airport?

 Match.

1. _d_ J Train   **a.** Downtown

2. ___ 12 Bus   **b.** Riverton Park

3. ___ 47 Bus   **c.** East Beach

4. ___ K Train   ~~**d.**~~ Riverton Airport

B   **Write.**

Kim: How do I get to East Beach?

Thomas: Take the _____ 12 Bus _____.

Kim: How do I get _____ Riverton Airport?

Thomas: Take the _____.

C   **Complete.**

| 7:30 | ~~does~~ | next | Thanks |

Marco: When _____ does _____ the _____ train to Dallas leave?

Woman: It leaves at _____.

Marco: At 7:30? _____.

A Read.

Ivan: Hello. My name is Ivan Stoli. I want a learner's permit.

Man: You need to take a test.

Ivan: Can I make an appointment for Tuesday?

Man: Yes. Can you come on Tuesday at 10:00?

Ivan: Tuesday at 10:00? That's fine.

Man: The test is $34.

Ivan: $34? Thank you.

B Circle.

1. Ivan wants _____.	a driver's license	(a learner's permit)
2. His appointment is _____.	Tuesday	Thursday
3. His appointment is at _____.	10:00	3:00
4. The test is _____.	$10	$34

C Read. Complete the form.

Ivan's full name is Ivan P. Stoli. His date of birth is September 15, 1982. He has blue eyes and blond hair. He wears glasses.

Application for a Learner's Permit

1. Name: <u>Stoli</u>
   (last)   (first)   (MI)

2. Date of birth: _____   5. ___ male   ___ female
   (MM/DD/YY)

3. Eye color: _____   6. Hair color: _____

4. Glasses? ___ yes ___ no

_____
(signature)

A Write.

| Bus Stop | ~~Hospital~~ | No Parking | One Way | Speed Limit | Stop |

1. Hospital

2. _____

3. _____

4. _____

5. _____

6. _____

B Circle the problem.

1.

a.
b.

2.

a.
b.

A **Complete.**

| does | every | hour | How | leave | minutes | often |

Marco: How often _____ does _____ the D Train leave?

Woman: It leaves _____ half hour.

Marco: Oh, good. At 2:00, 2:30, and 3:00.

Eva: _____ often does the subway leave?

Woman: It leaves every 15 _____.

Eva: Oh, good. At 12:00, 12:15, and 12:30.

Kim: How _____ does the bus _____?

Woman: It leaves every _____.

Kim: Oh, good. At 6:00, 7:00, and 8:00.

B **Circle.**

1. 3:00   3:30   4:00   4:30   every hour   (every half hour)

2. 4:15   5:15   6:15   7:15   every hour   every 15 minutes

3. 8:45   9:15   9:45   10:15   every half hour   every 15 minutes

4. 6:15   6:30   6:45   7:00   every half hour   every 15 minutes

5. 4:00   5:00   6:00   7:00   every hour   every half hour

Bus 25 leaves				
Beach Street	**Riverton Park**	**Riverton Library**	**Westside Hospital**	**Riverton Airport**
2:10		2:55	3:10	3:25
2:40	2:55	3:25	3:40	
3:10	3:25	3:55	4:10	4:35
3:40	3:55		4:20	4:55
5:00				6:10

B **Write.**

1. It's 3:20. When does the next bus leave Riverton Park? _____3:25_____

2. It's 5:55. When does the next bus leave Riverton Airport? _____

3. It's 3:10. When does the next bus leave Riverton Library? _____

4. It's 4:05. When does the next bus leave Westside Hospital? _____

5. It's 3:31. When does the next bus leave Beach Street? _____

A Write the words.

1. _____ a bus.
   e k a T

2. _____ a bike.
   d R e i

3. _____ a car.
   r e v i D

4. _____ a subway.
   k a e T

3. _____ a train.
   k e a T

4. _____ .
   k l a W

B The signs are wrong. Correct the signs.

A **Can/Can't**

Write *can* or *can't*.

1. Kim has a broken leg. She ____can't____ walk.

2. Luna has a stomachache. She _____ go to school today.

3. Thomas has a driver's license. He _____ drive a car.

4. Milly is two years old. She _____ drive.

5. Jane lives near a bus stop. She _____ take a bus to school.

6. Erik is from Brazil. He _____ speak Portuguese.

7. Soo Jin hurt his foot. He _____ play soccer.

8. Lin lives close to school. She _____ walk to school.

9. Jane has a bad cold. She _____ come to school today.

10. Eva's doctor works on Monday, Wednesday, Thursday, and Friday.

    Today is Tuesday. Eva _____ see her doctor today.

B **Complete with:** *in, next to, between*

Complete the sentences.

1. Thomas is _____ the restaurant.

2. The drugstore is _____ the restaurant.

3. The restaurant is _____ the bank and the drugstore.

C **Complete with:** *on, at*

Complete the sentences.

1. The party is _____on_____ Friday.

2. It's _____ 8:00 p.m.

3. My appointment is _____ Monday.

4. The restaurant closes _____ 11:00 p.m.

5. It closes _____ 9:00 p.m. _____ Sundays.

Unit 1

Student Book Pages	Workbook Pages
2	3
3	4-5
4	6
5	7
6	8-9
7	10
8	11
9	

Unit 2

Student Book Pages	Workbook Pages
11	15
12	16
13	17
14	18
15	19-21
16	22
17	23
18	

Unit 3

Student Book Pages	Workbook Pages
20	27-28
21	29
22	30
23	31
24	32-33
25	34
26	35
27	
28-29	38-39

Unit 4

Student Book Pages	Workbook Pages
31	43
32	44
33	45-46
34	47
35	48-49
36	50
37	51
38	

Unit 5

Student Book Pages	Workbook Pages
40	55
41	56-57
42	58-59
43	60
44	61
45	62
46	63
47	

Unit 6

Student Book Pages	Workbook Pages
49	67-68
50	69-70
51	71
52	72
53	73
54	74
55	75
56	
57-59	78-79

Unit 7

Student Book Pages	Workbook Pages
60	83
61	84-85
62	86-87
63	88
64	89
65	90
66	91
67	

Unit 8

Student Book Pages	Workbook Pages
69	95-96
70	97
71	98-99
72	100
73	101
74	102
75	103
76	

Unit 9

Student Book Pages	Workbook Pages
78	107
79	108
80	109
81	110-111
82	112-113
83	114
84	115
85	
86-87	118-119

Unit 10

Student Book Pages	Workbook Pages
89	123-124
90	125
91	126-127
92	128
93	129
94	130
95	131
96	

Unit 11

Student Book Pages	Workbook Pages
98	135
99	136-137
100	138-139
101	140
102	141
103	142
104	143
105	

Unit 12

Student Book Pages	Workbook Pages
107	147
108	148-149
109	150-151
110	152
111	153
112	154
113	155
114	
115-116	158-159